Disney

CAMP ROCK

ROCK STAR RECIPES

MEREDITH® BOOKS
DES MOINES, IA

Based on the Disney Channel Original Movie
"Camp Rock," Written by Karin Gist & Regina Hicks
and Julie Brown & Paul Brown

Meredith BOOKS

Meredith Books
1716 Locust Street
Des Moines, IA 50309-3023
meredithbooks.com

Printed in China.
First Edition.
ISBN: 978-0696-24294-6

Editor: Stephanie Karpinske, M.S., R.D.
Art Direction: Waterbury Publications, Inc., Ken Carlson

TABLE OF CONTENTS

CAMP COOKING CLASS

BEFORE YOU LEARN HOW TO PLAY AN INSTRUMENT, YOU HAVE TO LEARN THE BASICS, SUCH AS HOW TO READ MUSIC AND HOW TO HOLD AND PLAY THE INSTRUMENT. THE SAME IS TRUE FOR COOKING. YOU NEED TO LEARN THE BASICS FIRST AND THEN YOU CAN TRY MAKING A RECIPE. CONNIE, THE CAMP ROCK COOK (AND MITCHIE'S MOM), HAS PUT TOGETHER THIS LIST OF BASIC COOKING TIPS TO GET YOU STARTED.

BEFORE YOU START COOKING

⭐ Read the entire recipe from beginning to end with an adult. Ask yourself: Do I know exactly what I'm supposed to do? If there's anything you don't understand, ask an adult for help.

⭐ If you have any food allergies or intolerances, read the ingredients carefully to be sure all the foods are safe for you to eat.

⭐ Check your ingredients. Make sure you have enough of all the required ingredients. If you don't, make a list of the things you need and ask an adult to help you get them.

⭐ Check your utensils. Gather all the utensils and equipment you'll need to complete the recipe. If you're missing anything, ask an adult for help.

⭐ Always wash your hands with soap and water for at least 20 seconds before you start cooking.

SPECIAL INGREDIENT NOTES

⭐ Wash fresh fruits and veggies in cool water before eating or preparing them.

⭐ Only use clean, uncracked eggs.

WHEN COOKING YOUR (SOON TO BE) AWARD WINNING DISH

⭐ Measure ingredients accurately.

⭐ Follow the recipe step by step. Finish each step in the recipe before starting the next.

⭐ Use good food-safety habits. Cook and eat only fresh foods. After working with eggs, raw poultry, seafood, or meat, wash your hands, equipment, and any work surfaces.

⭐ Be safe. Children should not use knives or other sharp equipment without an adult's permission and supervision.

AT THE END OF YOUR SHOW-STOPPING MEAL

⭐ Put leftovers away as soon as possible. Leftovers should never sit out for more than 2 hours.

⭐ Put away all ingredients and equipment.

⭐ Clean up. Throw away trash such as food wrappers and empty packages. Load dirty dishes in the dishwasher or wash and dry them. Wipe counters and table with hot, soapy water.

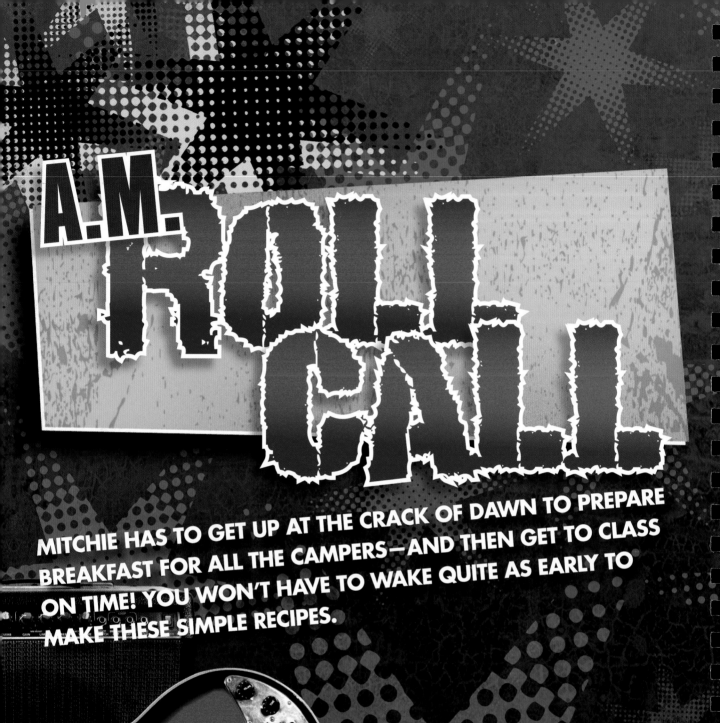

A.M. ROLL CALL

MITCHIE HAS TO GET UP AT THE CRACK OF DAWN TO PREPARE BREAKFAST FOR ALL THE CAMPERS—AND THEN GET TO CLASS ON TIME! YOU WON'T HAVE TO WAKE QUITE AS EARLY TO MAKE THESE SIMPLE RECIPES.

FRIES
WITH A DISGUISE

MITCHIE'S DISGUISE AS THE DAUGHTER OF A MUSIC INDUSTRY EXECUTIVE DIDN'T LAST LONG—AND NEITHER WILL THESE BAGEL FRIES!

UTENSILS

- Toaster
- Cutting board
- Serrated knife
- Large resealable plastic bag
- Measuring spoons

INGREDIENTS

1 4-inch whole wheat and/or cinnamon-raisin bagel, split in half

1 tablespoon butter, melted

1 tablespoon sugar

½ teaspoon ground cinnamon

DIRECTIONS

1 Toast the bagel halves in the toaster; let them cool a little. Place the bagel halves on the cutting board. Use the serrated knife to slice the bagel halves into ¼- to ½-inch-wide strips.

2 Put the bagel strips in the resealable plastic bag. Slowly pour melted butter over the bagel strips Seal the bag and shake to coat. Open the bag and sprinkle the sugar and cinnamon over the bagel strips. Reseal the bag and shake to coat again. Serve immediately. Makes 2 servings.

Nutrition Facts per serving: 192 calories, 6 g total fat, 15 mg cholesterol, 60 mg sodium, 30 g carbohydrate, 3 g fiber, 5 g protein.

MAKE IT YOURS USE FOUR SMALL WHOLE GRAIN WAFFLES IN PLACE OF THE BAGEL.

CAMP BREAKFAST COOKIES

WHEN YOU'RE RACING OFF TO VOICE LESSONS OR DANCE CLASS, GRAB ONE OF THESE CRUNCHY BREAKFAST COOKIES ON YOUR WAY OUT THE DOOR.

UTENSILS

- Cookie sheet
- Large mixing bowl
- Electric mixer
- Measuring cups
- Measuring spoons
- Wooden spoon
- Rubber scraper
- Hot pads
- Wide metal spatula
- Wire cooling rack

INGREDIENTS

Nonstick cooking spray
½ cup butter, softened
⅔ cup packed brown sugar
1 teaspoon baking soda
2 eggs
1¾ cups white whole wheat flour
3 cups multigrain cereal flakes with blueberries
½ cup raisins (optional)

DIRECTIONS

1 Turn on the oven to 350°F. Coat the cookie sheet with nonstick cooking spray. Save until Step 3.

2 Put the butter in the mixing bowl. Beat with the electric mixer for 30 seconds. Add brown sugar and baking soda. Beat until mixed. Add the eggs; beat until mixed. Add flour and beat until the mixture no longer looks dry. Use the wooden spoon to stir in the cereal and, if desired, raisins.

3 For each cookie, pack the mixture into a ¼-cup measuring cup. Use the rubber scraper to scrape it out of the cup onto the prepared cookie sheet. Press mound of dough to flatten it slightly. Repeat with remaining dough, placing cookies 3 inches apart.

4 Put the cookie sheet in the oven. Bake cookies for 8 minutes or until edges are golden brown. Turn off oven. Use hot pads to take the cookie sheet out of the oven. Let baked cookies stand on the cookie sheet for 1 minute. Use the spatula to transfer the cookies to the wire rack; let cookies cool. Makes 12 cookies.

Nutrition Facts per serving: 227 calories, 9 g total fat, 56 mg cholesterol, 228 mg sodium, 34 g carbohydrate, 1 g fiber, 4 g protein.

MAKE IT YOURS INSTEAD OF MULTIGRAIN CEREAL FLAKES WITH BLUBERRIES, TRY BRAN CEREAL FLAKES WITH RAISINS.

LET'S JAM MUFFINS

YOU'LL HAVE THE ENERGY TO JAM FOR HOURS WHEN YOU FILL UP ON THESE TASTY MUFFINS.

UTENSILS

- Muffin pan with twelve 2½-inch cups
- Measuring cups
- Measuring spoons
- Large mixing bowl
- Wooden spoon
- Medium mixing bowl
- Wooden toothpicks
- Hot pads
- Wire cooling rack

INGREDIENTS

1¾ cups all-purpose flour
⅓ cup packed brown sugar
1½ teaspoons baking powder
½ teaspoon baking soda
1 teaspoon apple pie spice
¼ teaspoon salt
½ of a 17-ounce can sweet potatoes, drained (about 1 cup)
1 egg, beaten
½ cup milk
⅓ cup strawberry fruit jam or preserves
¼ cup cooking oil

DIRECTIONS

1 Turn on the oven to 400°F. Line twelve 2½-inch muffin cups with paper bake cups. Save until Step 4.

2 Put flour, brown sugar, baking powder, baking soda, apple pie spice, and salt in the large bowl. Stir with the wooden spoon to mix.

3 Place the drained sweet potatoes in the medium bowl. Use the fork to mash up the sweet potatoes. Add the egg, milk, jam, and oil to the sweet potatoes. Beat with the fork until ingredients are well mixed.

4 Add the sweet potato mixture to flour mixture. Stir with the wooden spoon until dry ingredients are wet. Spoon some of the batter into each muffin cup.

5 Put muffin pan in oven. Bake 18 to 20 minutes or until muffins are golden and a wooden toothpick comes out clean. (To test for doneness, use hot pads to pull out oven rack. Stick a toothpick into the center of one of the muffins; pull out toothpick. If any muffin sticks to it, carefully push the oven rack back into place using hot pads and bake the muffins a few minutes more; test again.) Turn off oven.

6 Use hot pads to remove muffin pan from the oven. Place muffin pan on the cooling rack and let cool for 5 minutes. Tip muffin pan to carefully remove muffins onto the cooling rack. Cool muffins on cooling rack about 10 minutes. If desired, top with additional jam or preserves. Makes 12 muffins.

Nutrition Facts per serving: 182 calories, 5 g total fat, 18 mg cholesterol, 153 mg sodium, 31 g carbohydrate, 1 g fiber, 3 g protein.

MAKE IT YOURS TRY A DIFFERENT FRUIT JAM OR PRESERVE SUCH AS PLUM, PEACH, OR APRICOT.

ROCK AND (CINNAMON) ROLL OATMEAL

PLAIN OATMEAL IS BORING, BUT IT ROCKS WHEN YOU MAKE IT TASTE LIKE A CINNAMON ROLL.

UTENSILS

- Microwave-safe bowl
- Measuring cups
- Hot pads
- Wooden spoon
- Measuring spoons

INGREDIENTS

1 envelope (0.98-ounce) plain instant oatmeal

⅔ cup water

1 tablespoon tub-style light cream cheese

¼ teaspoon ground cinnamon

2 tablespoons raisins (optional)

Ground cinnamon (optional)

DIRECTIONS

1 Open oatmeal envelope. Pour oatmeal into a microwave-safe bowl. Add the water to the oatmeal. Place bowl in microwave oven; close door. Microwave on 100% power (high) for 1 to 2 minutes or until thickened. Use hot pads to remove bowl from the microwave. Stir with the wooden spoon until mixed. Add cream cheese and ¼ teaspoon cinnamon to oatmeal; stir until mixed. If desired, add raisins and sprinkle with additional cinnamon. Makes 1 serving.

Nutrition Facts per serving: 136 calories, 4 g total fat, 8 mg cholesterol, 152 mg sodium, 20 g carbohydrate, 3 g fiber, 5 g protein.

MAKE IT YOURS TRY DRIED CHERRIES, BLUEBERRIES, OR CRANBERRIES IN YOUR OATMEAL INSTEAD OF THE RAISINS.

HAM IT UP WAFFLEWICH

TO "HAM IT UP" ONSTAGE MEANS TO DO A PERFORMANCE THAT'S A LITTLE OVER THE TOP FOR WHAT'S EXPECTED. IF YOU PREFER TO LEAVE THE HAM ON YOUR PLATE, YOU'LL LOVE THESE BREAKFAST SANDWICHES.

UTENSILS

- Toaster
- Table knife
- Measuring spoons
- Microwave-safe plate
- Hot pads
- Fork

INGREDIENTS

2 frozen whole grain waffles

1 tablespoon tub-style light cream cheese

1 tablespoon cherry or strawberry preserves

1 ounce thinly sliced cooked ham

Maple syrup (optional)

Apple slices sprinkled with ground cinnamon (optional)

DIRECTIONS

1 Toast the waffles in the toaster until golden. Spread 1 waffle with cream cheese and the other with preserves.

2 Place the ham on the microwave-safe plate. Put ham in microwave oven; close door. Microwave ham on 100% power (high) for 10 seconds. Using hot pads, remove the plate from the microwave oven. Use a fork to put the ham on top of 1 waffle. Top with remaining waffle, spread side down. If desired, serve with syrup and garnish with apple slices sprinkled with cinnamon. Makes 1 serving.

Nutrition Facts per serving: 274 calories, 7 g total fat, 24 mg cholesterol, 881 mg sodium, 44 g carbohydrate, 3 g fiber, 11 g protein.

MAKE IT YOURS TRY USING APPLE-CINNAMON WAFFLES INSTEAD OF THE WHOLE GRAIN WAFFLES.

17

PERFECT TRIO
EGG MUFFIN

A GROUP OF THREE PERFORMERS, LIKE CONNECT 3, MAKES FOR A GOOD BAND. THE RULE OF THREE HOLDS TRUE FOR THESE SANDWICHES AS WELL. BREAD, EGGS, AND CHEESE COMBINE TO MAKE A DELICIOUS TRIO.

UTENSILS

- Glass measuring cup
- Measuring spoons
- Fork
- Hot pads
- Microwave-safe plate

INGREDIENTS

1 egg
1 tablespoon lowfat milk
1 whole grain English muffin, split in half and toasted
1 slice American cheese

DIRECTIONS

1 Crack egg into the measuring cup. Add milk. Beat egg and milk with the fork until mixture is pale yellow and the yolk is completely broken. Put the measuring cup into the microwave oven; close the door. Microwave on high for 25 seconds. Use hot pads to remove measuring cup from microwave. Stir with fork. Microwave on high for 20 seconds more. Egg should be slightly firm but not runny. Use hot pads to remove from microwave.

2 Top one of the English muffin halves with cooked egg and cheese. Top with the other half of the English muffin. Place sandwich on microwave-safe plate. Microwave on high for 30 seconds or until cheese melts. Use hot pads to remove from microwave. Makes 1 serving.

Nutrition Facts per serving: 305 calories, 14 g total fat, 235 mg cholesterol, 747 mg sodium, 30 g carbohydrate, 4 g fiber, 18 g protein.

MAKE IT YOURS WRAP UP THE EGG AND CHEESE IN A WHOLE WHEAT FLOUR TORTILLA INSTEAD OF PUTTING IT ON AN ENGLISH MUFFIN.

ACT COOL QUESADILLAS

THESE NO-MESS QUESADILLAS WILL HELP YOU APPEAR "TOO COOL" WHENEVER A SUPERSTAR LIKE SHANE WALKS BY.

UTENSILS

- Measuring spoons
- Small mixing bowl
- Wooden spoon
- Table knife
- Sharp knife

INGREDIENTS

½ of an 8-ounce tub light cream cheese, softened

½ teaspoon finely shredded orange peel

2 to 3 teaspoons low-fat milk

3 8-inch whole wheat flour tortillas

2 medium green or red apples, cored and thinly sliced

¼ cup chopped almonds, pecans, or walnuts, toasted, if desired (optional)

DIRECTIONS

1 Place the cream cheese, orange peel, and 2 teaspoons milk in the small bowl. Use the wooden spoon to stir until well mixed. If it's too thick to spread, add another teaspoon of milk and stir to mix. Use the table knife to spread one side of each tortilla with the cream cheese mixture.

2 On 1 tortilla, arrange half of the apple slices. If desired, sprinkle with half of the almonds. Top with another tortilla, cream cheese side up. Top with remaining apple slices and, if desired, almonds. Top with remaining tortilla, cream cheese side down. Cut into wedges with the sharp knife. Makes 4 servings.

Nutrition Facts per serving: 188 calories, 7 g total fat, 13 mg cholesterol, 375 mg sodium, 23 g carbohydrate, 9 g fiber, 9 g protein.

MAKE IT YOURS SWITCH OUT THE APPLE FOR A PEAR, OR PEEL AND SLICE ONE BANANA.

LATE FOR CLASS SMOOTHIES

BEING LATE FOR CLASS IS NOT THE WAY TO MAKE A GOOD IMPRESSION. THIS QUICK-TO-FIX DRINK WILL HELP YOU GET THERE ON TIME.

UTENSILS

- Measuring cups
- Electric blender
- 2 serving glasses
- Rubber scraper

INGREDIENTS

1 cup hulled and chopped fresh strawberries

1 cup peeled and sliced banana

1 cup low-fat milk

1 cup low-fat yogurt (plain, flavored, or frozen)

Fresh whole strawberries (optional)

DIRECTIONS

1 Put strawberries, sliced banana, milk, and yogurt in the blender.

2 Cover the blender with the lid and blend on high speed until the mixture is smooth. Turn off the blender. Pour mixture into the serving glasses. Use the rubber scraper to get all of the drink out of the blender. If desired, top the drinks with strawberries.

NOTE* Frozen fruit makes a thicker, slushier smoothie. If you are using fresh fruit but want that texture, add a few ice cubes to the blender. Makes 2 servings.

Nutrition Facts per serving: 218 calories, 4 g total fat, 13 mg cholesterol, 141 mg sodium, 37 g carbohydrate, 4 g fiber, 12 g protein.

MAKE IT YOURS MIX YOUR OWN SMOOTHIE INGREDIENTS. TRY PEACHES AND RASPBERRIES WITH VANILLA LOW-FAT YOGURT OR PINEAPPLE WITH STRAWBERRY LOW-FAT YOGURT.

BREAK FOR LUNCH

A MORNING OF SINGING, DANCING, AND WRITING SONGS CAN MAKE A CAMPER HUNGRY. AFTER YOUR BUSY MORNING, TAKE A BREAK WITH A CRUNCHY SALAD, SATISFYING SANDWICH, OR OTHER MESS HALL FAVORITES.

SHAKE IT! SALAD

IN HIP-HOP CLASS, SHANE SHOWS OFF HIS MOVES FOR THE CAMPERS. PRACTICE YOUR MOVES BY SHAKING UP THIS SIMPLE SALAD.

UTENSILS

- Cutting board
- Sharp knife
- Measuring cups
- 4-cup plastic storage container with lid or 1-quart resealable plastic bag
- Measuring spoons
- Small plastic storage container with lid

INGREDIENTS

¼ of a small cucumber

¼ cup grape or cherry tomatoes

1 ounce cooked chicken

1 cup torn mixed salad greens

2 tablespoons shredded mozzarella cheese

1 tablespoon sliced almonds or walnut pieces (optional)

2 tablespoons of your favorite bottled reduced-fat or reduced-calorie salad dressing

DIRECTIONS

1 Put the cucumber on the cutting board. Use the sharp knife to cut the cucumber into thin slices. On the same cutting board, use the sharp knife to cut the tomatoes in half and the chicken into ½-inch pieces.

2 Put the salad greens in the 4-cup plastic container (or 1-quart resealable plastic bag). Put the lid on the container and seal, or seal the bag. Put the cucumber, tomato, chicken, cheese, and, if desired, the nuts in separate small resealable plastic bags and seal. Put the salad dressing in the small plastic container. Put the lid on the container and seal. Chill all ingredients for up to 4 hours.

3 When ready to eat, uncover all ingredients. Add the cucumber, tomato, chicken, cheese, nuts (if using), and dressing to the salad greens. Put the lid on the container and seal, or seal the bag. Shake to mix. Makes 1 serving.

Nutrition Facts per serving: 175 calories, 11 g total fat, 35 mg cholesterol, 535 mg sodium, 8 g carbohydrate, 2 g fiber, 13 g protein.

MAKE IT YOURS USE COOKED TURKEY OR HAM IN PLACE OF THE CHICKEN.

HOT TUNES TUNA

UNLIKE MITCHIE'S STORY ABOUT HER MOM WORKING FOR HOT TUNES TV, THERE'S NO LIE ABOUT THIS SANDWICH. IT'S ONE OF THE BEST EVER!

UTENSILS

- Can opener
- Small bowl
- Spoon
- Measuring cups
- Table knife

INGREDIENTS

1 12-ounce can chunk white tuna (water-pack), drained and flaked

⅓ cup bottled reduced-calorie ranch salad dressing

⅓ cup finely chopped fresh or drained, canned pineapple

¼ cup finely chopped red sweet pepper

4 mini whole wheat bagel squares

4 lettuce leaves

DIRECTIONS

1 In the small bowl use the spoon to combine tuna and salad dressing. Gently stir in the pineapple and the sweet pepper.

2 Spread tuna mixture on the bagel bottoms using the table knife. Top with lettuce leaves and bagel tops. Makes 4 servings.

Nutrition Facts per serving: 304 calories, 7 g total fat, 43 mg cholesterol, 823 mg sodium, 35 g carbohydrate, 5 g fiber, 27 g protein.

MAKE IT YOURS USE TWO WHOLE WHEAT PITA BREAD ROUNDS, HALVED INSTEAD OF THE BAGEL SQUARES. PLACE THE LETTUCE IN THE PITA HALVES AND FILL EACH WITH TUNA MIXTURE.

PICNIC BY THE LAKE SALAD

WHEN SHANE AND MITCHIE HANG OUT BY THE LAKE, THEY BECOME FRIENDS. AND THIS CHICKEN SALAD MAKES FOR PERFECT PICNIC FOOD.

UTENSILS

- Measuring cups
- Measuring spoons
- Medium mixing bowl
- Wooden spoon
- Airtight storage container

INGREDIENTS

½ cup low-fat mayonnaise

1 tablespoon lemon juice

2½ cups chopped cooked chicken or turkey

¼ cup grated Parmesan cheese

¼ cup finely chopped celery

Shredded lettuce (optional)

Baked scoop-shaped tortilla chips (optional)

DIRECTIONS

1 Put mayonnaise and lemon juice in the bowl. Use the wooden spoon to combine. Add the chicken, Parmesan cheese, and celery. Stir to combine. Put chicken mixture in the airtight container and chill 1 to 4 hours.

2 If desired, serve the chicken salad on top of the shredded lettuce and use tortilla chips to scoop up the salad. Makes 6 main-dish servings.

Nutrition Facts per serving: 193 calories, 12 g total fat, 62 mg cholesterol, 264 mg sodium, 2 g carbohydrate, 0 g fiber, 18 g protein.

MAKE IT YOURS INSTEAD OF USING MAYONNAISE AND LEMON JUICE IN THE SALAD, USE ½ CUP OF REDUCED-CALORIE RANCH SALAD DRESSING.

THAT'S A WRAP

SANDER LOVES TO RAP AND MAKE UP HIS OWN HIT SONGS. YOU CAN WRAP UP A HIT TOO WHEN YOU MAKE THESE FAJITA ROLL-UPS.

UTENSILS

- Foil
- Hot pads
- 12-inch nonstick skillet
- Wooden spoon
- Colander
- Medium mixing bowl
- Slotted spoon
- Cutting board
- Serrated knife

INGREDIENTS

2 10-inch whole wheat tortillas
Nonstick cooking spray
12 ounces packaged chicken strips
1 small red or green sweet pepper, seeded and cut into thin strips
½ teaspoon chili powder
¼ teaspoon garlic powder
2 tablespoons bottled reduced-calorie ranch salad dressing
½ cup refrigerated fresh salsa
⅓ cup reduced-fat shredded cheese
Refrigerated fresh salsa (optional)

DIRECTIONS

1 Turn on oven to 350°F. Wrap tortillas tightly in foil. and put in oven. Bake 10 minutes. Use hot pads to remove the tortillas from the oven. Turn off oven.

2 Spray the nonstick skillet with cooking spray. Put skillet on a burner. Turn burner to medium-high heat. Add half of the chicken. Cook and stir with the wooden spoon for 2 to 3 minutes or until chicken is no longer pink. Put the colander over the bowl. Use the slotted spoon to remove chicken from skillet and put in colander. Add remaining chicken, sweet pepper, chili powder, and garlic powder to the skillet. Cook and stir for 2 to 3 minutes or until chicken is no longer pink, stirring the chicken all the time with the wooden spoon. Turn off burner. Spoon meat and vegetables into the colander along with liquid from skillet. Let the liquid drain into the bowl. Put the liquid in a container to throw away. Put all of the chicken mixture back in the medium bowl and stir in the salad dressing.

3 To serve, place a warm tortilla on the cutting board. Spoon half of the chicken mixture along one edge of the tortilla. Top with half of the salsa and cheese. Roll up tortilla. Use the serrated knife to cut in half. Repeat with remaining tortilla, chicken, salsa, and cheese. If desired, top with additional salsa. Makes 4 servings.

Nutrition Facts per serving: 247 calories, 8 g total fat, 62 mg cholesterol, 502 mg sodium, 15 g carbohydrate, 1 g fiber, 27 g protein.

MAKE IT YOURS USE 12 OUNCES PACKAGED BEEF STIR-FRY STRIPS IN PLACE OF THE CHICKEN.

33

VIP SECTION
SANDWICHES

THE QUEEN BEES HAVE TO BE BETTER THAN EVERYONE ELSE, SO IT'S NO WONDER THAT THEY PREFER THIS MORE SOPHISTICATED GRILLED CHEESE SANDWICH OVER THE TRADITIONAL VERSION.

UTENSILS

- Table knife
- Measuring spoons
- Measuring cups
- Shallow bowl or pie plate
- Whisk
- Nonstick griddle
- Pancake turner
- Hot pads

INGREDIENTS

2 to 3 teaspoons Dijon-style mustard
4 slices firm wheat bread
2 ounces thinly sliced cooked ham
2 slices Swiss cheese
¼ cup low-fat milk
1 egg white
Nonstick cooking spray

DIRECTIONS

1 Use the knife to spread the mustard on 2 of the bread slices. Top mustard with ham and cheese. Place remaining bread slices on top of the ham and cheese. Put the milk and egg white in the shallow bowl or pie plate. Whisk until well mixed.

2 Coat an unheated nonstick griddle with nonstick cooking spray. Put griddle on burner. Turn burner to medium heat. Dip each sandwich in milk mixture and turn to coat both sides. Put sandwiches on the hot griddle. Cook for 1 to 2 minutes or until bottoms are golden brown. Use the pancake turner to turn sandwiches over. Cook for 1 to 2 minutes more or until golden brown and cheese is melted. Turn off burner. Use the hot pads to remove griddle from burner. Use the pancake turner to remove the sandwiches from the griddle. Makes 2 servings.

Nutrition Facts per serving: 313 calories, 13 g total fat, 44 mg cholesterol, 846 mg sodium, 28 g carbohydrate, 2 g fiber, 21 g protein.

MAKE IT YOURS USE TWO SLICES AMERICAN CHEESE FOR THE SWISS CHEESE.

35

MESS HALL
MAC N CHEESE

WHILE ON KITCHEN DUTY, MITCHIE SPENT HOURS STIRRING HER MOM'S MACARONI AND CHEESE. GOOD THING CAITLYN WAS THERE FOR SOME COMPANY! MAKE THIS WITH YOUR FRIEND AND ENJOY IT TOGETHER.

UTENSILS

- Measuring cups
- Large saucepan
- Wooden spoon
- Hot pads
- Colander
- Measuring spoons
- Medium saucepan

INGREDIENTS

1⅓ cups dried multigrain elbow macaroni

2 tablespoons all-purpose flour

¼ teaspoon salt

1 cup lowfat milk

10 slices reduced-fat American cheese, torn

DIRECTIONS

1 Cook macaroni in the large saucepan following the package directions. When the macaroni is cooked, turn off burner. Using hot pads, remove saucepan from burner. Place colander in sink. Carefully pour macaroni into the colander to drain water. Save until Step 2.

2 Stir the flour and salt together in the medium saucepan. Stir in the milk until mixture is smooth. Put saucepan on a burner. Turn the burner to medium heat. Cook and stir until thickened and bubbly. Turn the burner to low heat. Add the cheese and continue to stir until melted. Stir in the cooked macaroni and heat through. Turn off burner. Use hot pads to remove saucepan from burner. Makes 4 servings.

Nutrition Facts per serving: 281 calories, 8 g total fat, 29 mg cholesterol, 962 mg sodium, 38 g carbohydrate, 3 g fiber, 16 g protein.

MAKE IT YOURS USE DRIED MULTIGRAIN CORKSCREW PASTA FOR A FUN "TWIST."

CHILI
FOR A CROWD

CHILI IS A FAVORITE FOOD AT CAMP, BUT CONNIE HAD TO SEARCH HER COOKBOOKS TO FIND A RECIPE TO FEED 300! THIS SUPER-SIMPLE CHILI IS MUCH EASIER—IT ONLY MAKES ENOUGH FOR SIX HUNGRY CAMPERS.

UTENSILS

- Large skillet with lid
- Wooden spoon
- Colander
- Medium bowl
- Hot pads
- Wire cooling rack
- Large spoon
- Disposable container
- Measuring cups
- Measuring spoons

INGREDIENTS

12 ounces lean ground beef
1 15-ounce can pinto beans, rinsed and drained
1 cup bottled salsa
½ cup water
1 teaspoon chili powder
Light dairy sour cream (optional)

DIRECTIONS

1 Put ground beef in the large skillet. Break up meat with the wooden spoon. Put the skillet on burner. Turn burner to medium-high heat. Cook until no pink color is left in the meat, stirring now and then with the wooden spoon. This will take 8 to 10 minutes. Put colander over the bowl. Turn off burner. Use hot pads to remove skillet from burner. Place on cooling rack. Spoon meat and juices into the colander and let the fat drain into the bowl. Spoon meat back into skillet. Put cooled fat in a container and throw away.

2 Stir beans, salsa, water, and chili powder into meat in skillet. Put skillet on burner. Turn burner to medium-high heat. Bring to boiling. Turn down heat to low. Cover skillet with lid. Cook about 10 minutes or until everything is hot. Turn off burner. Use hot pads to remove skillet from burner. If desired, serve with sour cream. Makes 6 servings.

Nutrition Facts per serving: 174 calories, 6 g total fat, 37 mg cholesterol, 507 mg sodium, 14 g carbohydrate, 4 g fiber, 15 g protein.

MAKE IT YOURS REPLACE THE GROUND BEEF WITH GROUND TURKEY.

FIND YOUR STYLE SPUDS

AS CAMP DIRECTOR BROWN CESARIO WOULD SAY, CAMP ROCK IS ALL ABOUT FINDING YOUR STYLE. THIS BAKED POTATO BAR LETS YOU DO THE SAME. PICK YOUR TOPPINGS TO CREATE YOUR OWN UNIQUE MEAL.

UTENSILS

- Vegetable brush
- Fork
- Spoon
- Measuring cups
- Wooden spoon
- Small saucepan
- Hot pads
- Sharp knife

INGREDIENTS

4 large baking potatoes (about 2 pounds)

1 8-ounce container light dairy sour cream ranch-flavor dip

1 cup diced cooked turkey ham

½ cup reduced-fat shredded cheddar cheese

Chopped tomato (optional)

Snipped chives (optional)

DIRECTIONS

1 Scrub potatoes with a vegetable brush. Use the fork to poke potatoes in several places.

2 Place poked potatoes on a microwave-safe plate and put into the microwave; close door. Microwave on 100% power (high) for 15 to 20 minutes or until almost tender, rearranging once. Let potatoes stand for 5 minutes before cutting them open and adding the toppings.

3 While potatoes are cooking, spoon dip into the small saucepan. Stir in the ham and cheese. Put saucepan on a burner. Turn burner to medium-low heat. Cook until mixture is hot, stirring now and then with a wooden spoon. Turn off burner. Use hot pads to remove saucepan from burner.

4 Use hot pads to remove potatoes from the microwave. Use the knife to cut a cross or a small oval in the top of each potato. Push ends of each potato toward center to make an opening.

5 Spoon some of the sour cream dip mixture over each potato. If desired, sprinkle with tomato and chives. Makes 4 servings.

Nutrition Facts per serving: 338 calories, 9 g total fat, 51 mg cholesterol, 798 mg sodium, 47 g carbohydrate, 4 g fiber, 19 g protein.

MAKE IT YOURS
USE SWEET POTATOES INSTEAD OF THE BAKING POTATOES.

Ranch-style: Measure ¾ cup bottled reduced-fat ranch salad dressing and 4 tablespoons cooked turkey bacon pieces. Spoon some of the ranch dressing on each baked potato. Sprinkle 1 tablespoon cooked turkey bacon pieces on top of ranch dressing on each potato.

Chili-style: Measure 1 cup canned vegetarian chili with beans. Put in a small saucepan. Put saucepan on a burner. Turn burner to medium-low heat. Cook until chili is hot, stirring now and then with a wooden spoon. Turn off burner. Use a hot pad to remove saucepan from heat. Spoon ¼ cup chili over each baked potato. Spoon 1 tablespoon light dairy sour cream over chili on each baked potato.

REHEARSAL SNACKS

WHY SETTLE FOR PLAIN OLD CHIPS OR CANDY WHEN YOU CAN SHOW YOUR STYLE WITH A SNACK THAT'S ALL YOU? WHETHER YOU PICK POPCORN, A SAVORY CEREAL MIX, OR A SLUSHY DRINK, THESE SNACKS WILL HAVE YOU ROCKIN' UNTIL YOUR NEXT MEAL.

BAG A HIT CHIPS

CAITLYN IS DETERMINED TO PRODUCE A BEST-SELLING CD AND PROVE TO TESS AND THE OTHER CAMPERS THAT SHE CAN DO IT. YOU CAN BAG A HIT AT SNACK TIME BY SERVING UP THESE TO YOUR FRIENDS.

UTENSILS

- Measuring spoons
- Microwave-safe custard cup
- Waxed paper
- Hot pads
- Scissors
- Small spoon

INGREDIENTS

2 tablespoons purchased pizza sauce

1 100-calorie package cheese-flavored crisps

1 tablespoon shredded part-skim mozzarella cheese

DIRECTIONS

1 Put pizza sauce in the custard cup. Cover with waxed paper. Put in microwave oven; close door. Cook at 100% power (high) about 20 seconds or until warm. Use hot pads to remove the custard cup from the microwave.

2 Open the package of cheese crisps. Use the scissors to cut off more of the top of the package to make it easier to eat with a spoon. Spoon pizza sauce over crisps in bag. Sprinkle with cheese. Makes 1 serving.

Nutrition Facts per serving: 133 calories, 4 g total fat, 5 mg cholesterol, 423 mg sodium, 19 g carbohydrate, 2 g fiber, 4 g protein.

MAKE IT YOURS FOR A PORTABLE TACO, MAKE AS DIRECTED ABOVE, EXCEPT USE SALSA INSTEAD OF PIZZA SAUCE AND SHREDDED REDUCED-FAT CHEDDAR CHEESE INSTEAD OF MOZZARELLA CHEESE.

STRIKE A CHORD SNACK

LEARNING TO PLAY GUITAR, OR ANY INSTRUMENT, TAKES LOTS OF PRACTICE, SO KEEP UP YOUR ENERGY WITH THIS PORTABLE SNACK MIX.

UTENSILS

- Measuring cups
- Large bowl
- Small bowl
- Measuring spoons
- Wooden spoon
- Large roasting pan
- Hot pads
- Foil
- Airtight storage container

INGREDIENTS

4 cups bite-size shredded wheat biscuits

1 ½ cups mini bagel chips

1 ½ cups peanuts or whole almonds

3 tablespoons butter, melted

1 tablespoon lime juice

1 teaspoon garlic powder

½ teaspoon chili powder

½ teaspoon onion salt

DIRECTIONS

1 Turn on the oven to 300°F. Put shredded wheat biscuits, bagel chips, and peanuts in the large bowl.

2 In the small bowl combine the melted butter, lime juice, garlic powder, chili powder, and onion salt. Stir with the wooden spoon to combine. Pour the melted butter mixture over the cereal mixture. Use the wooden spoon to combine. Place the cereal mixture in the roasting pan. Place the pan in the oven. Bake for 10 minutes. Use the hot pads to remove the pan from the oven. Use the wooden spoon to stir the mixture. Use the hot pads to return the pan to the oven. Bake for 10 minutes more. Turn off the oven. Use the hot pads to remove the pan from the oven.

3 Pour the mixture on the foil to cool. Store in the airtight container at room temperature up to 2 weeks. Makes about 8 cups.

Nutrition Facts per ½-cup serving: 150 calories, 10 g total fat, 6 mg cholesterol, 101 mg sodium, 14 g carbohydrate, 2 g fiber, 5 g protein.

MAKE IT YOURS REPLACE THE MINI BAGEL CHIPS WITH 1 ½ CUPS PRETZEL TWISTS.

THE QUEEN BEE MIX

SWEET FRUIT AND CRUNCHY NUTS COMBINE TO MAKE THIS TASTY TRAIL MIX THAT WOULD PLEASE EVEN THE QUEEN BEES.

UTENSILS

- Measuring cups
- Medium bowl
- Wooden spoon
- 4 small resealable plastic bags

DIRECTIONS

1 Put dried apples, grapes, blueberries, raisins, and peanuts in the bowl. Use the wooden spoon to combine. Divide fruit mixture evenly among plastic bags. Makes 4 servings.

Nutrition Facts per serving: 170 calories, 5 g total fat, 0 mg cholesterol, 49 mg sodium, 32 g carbohydrate, 4 g fiber, 3 g protein.

INGREDIENTS

1 cup dried apples
1 cup seedless red or green grapes
½ cup fresh blueberries
¼ cup raisins
¼ cup peanuts

MAKE IT YOURS TRY USING DRIED CHERRIES OR DRIED CRANBERRIES INSTEAD OF THE RAISINS.

48

FIT FOR THE STAGE VEGGIES

TESS BELIEVES HEALTHFUL VEGGIES KEEP HER BODY IN TOP SHAPE FOR PERFORMING ONSTAGE. ALONG WITH DIP, THEY MAKE A GREAT SNACK!

UTENSILS

- Measuring spoons
- 1 plastic drinking cup
- 1 small spoon
- Measuring cups

INGREDIENTS

3 tablespoons light dairy sour cream

⅛ teaspoon dried dillweed

½ cup vegetable sticks* (carrots, red sweet pepper, and/or cucumber)

DIRECTIONS

1 Place sour cream and dillweed into the bottom of a plastic drinking cup. Use spoon to stir to combine. Insert vegetable sticks into dip in cup.

NOTE* Look for precut vegetable sticks in the produce aisle of your supermarket. Makes 1 serving.

Nutrition Facts per serving: 74 calories, 4 g total fat, 13 mg cholesterol, 68 mg sodium, 8 g carbohydrate, 2 g fiber, 2 g protein.

MAKE IT YOURS REPLACE DRIED DILLWEED WITH DRIED ITALIAN SEASONING OR DRIED BASIL.

49

KEEP THE BEAT STICKS

YOU CAN PRACTICE KEEPING THE BEAT WITH THESE CRUNCHY, FLAVORED PRETZEL STICKS.

UTENSILS

- 14x12-inch piece of waxed paper
- Measuring cups
- Measuring spoons
- Table knife
- Airtight container with lid

INGREDIENTS

¾ cup round toasted oat cereal with nuts and honey

2 tablespoons creamy peanut butter

4 long pretzel sticks

DIRECTIONS

1 Lay the waxed paper on the counter. Spread cereal on waxed paper. Set aside.

2 Using the table knife, spread peanut butter in a thin layer over half of each pretzel stick. Roll each stick in the cereal so it sticks to the peanut butter. Eat right away or put sticks in an airtight container and store at room temperature for up to 1 day. Makes 4 servings.

Nutrition Facts per serving: 106 calories, 5 g total fat, 0 mg cholesterol, 198 mg sodium, 13 g carbohydrate, 1 g fiber, 4 g protein.

MAKE IT YOURS USE APPLE-AND-CINNAMON-FLAVORED ROUND TOASTED CEREAL IN PLACE OF THE CEREAL WITH NUTS AND HONEY.

PAJAMA JAM POPCORN

SIT BACK AND ENJOY THE PAJAMA JAM PERFORMERS WHILE YOU SNACK ON THIS SWEET POPCORN MIX.

UTENSILS

- Measuring cups
- Measuring spoons
- 5- to 6-quart pot
- Wooden spoon
- Hot pads
- Large baking sheets
- Waxed paper or parchment paper
- Storage container with lid

INGREDIENTS

1¼ cups sugar
¼ cup water
2 tablespoons butter
⅛ teaspoon ground cinnamon
8 cups popped popcorn
1 cup peanuts
1 cup golden raisins

DIRECTIONS

1 Put sugar, water, butter, and cinnamon in the pot. Put pot on a burner. Turn burner to medium heat. Cook and stir with the wooden spoon until the mixture comes to a boil. Cook for 5 minutes more, stirring occasionally with the wooden spoon. Turn off burner. Use hot pads to remove pot from burner.

2 Add the popcorn, peanuts, and raisins to the syrup; stir quickly with the wooden spoon to coat all ingredients evenly. Spread coated popcorn mixture in a single layer on 1 or 2 large baking sheets lined with waxed paper or parchment paper. Cool completely. Break up any large pieces. Store in an airtight container at room temperature for up to 3 days. Makes about 12 cups.

Nutrition Facts per ½-cup serving: 117 calories, 4 g total fat, 3 mg cholesterol, 28 mg sodium, 19 g carbohydrate, 1 g fiber, 2 g protein.

MAKE IT YOURS REPLACE THE PEANUTS WITH CASHEWS OR ALMONDS AND USE MIXED DRIED FRUIT BITS INSTEAD OF RAISINS.

PRACTICE MAKES PERFECT
MICROPOPS

PRACTICE FOR OPEN MIC NIGHT WITH THESE FROZEN POPS. BUT MAKE IT QUICK—THEY MAY MELT AFTER THE FIRST SONG!

UTENSILS

- Measuring cups
- Electric blender
- 12 frozen treat molds or twelve 4- to 6-ounce paper cups
- Foil (if using paper cups)
- Sharp knife (if using paper cups)
- 12 pop sticks (if using paper cups)

INGREDIENTS

1 cup guava nectar
1 cup unsweetened pineapple juice
1 cup fresh pineapple chunks
1 cup coarsely chopped or sliced fresh strawberries

DIRECTIONS

1 Put the guava nectar, pineapple juice, and fresh pineapple chunks in the blender. Cover the blender with the lid and blend on high speed until smooth. Turn off the blender. Divide chopped or sliced strawberries among the frozen treat molds or 4- to 6-ounce paper cups. Pour the blended mixture over the fruit.

2 Add handles and cover the frozen treat molds. (Or cover each paper cup with foil. Make a small hole in the foil with the knife. Insert a pop stick into the cup through hole.) Freeze about 4 hours or until firm. Remove from the freezer. Remove the pops from the molds or remove the foil and tear paper cups away. Makes 12 pops.

Nutrition Facts per serving: 36 calories, 0 g total fat, 0 mg cholesterol, 1 mg sodium, 9 g carbohydrate, 1 g fiber, 0 g protein.

MAKE IT YOURS USE PEELED AND COARSELY CHOPPED OR SLICED KIWIFRUIT OR PAPAYA INSTEAD OF THE STRAWBERRIES.

SUPERSTAR SLUSHES

AFTER A NIGHT OF SINGING, TRY THIS ICY DRINK. IT'S FULL OF LEMON AND HONEY, WHICH CAN SOOTHE A SINGER'S SCRATCHY THROAT.

UTENSILS

- Measuring cups
- Measuring spoons
- Electric blender
- 4 serving glasses
- Rubber scraper

INGREDIENTS

- 2 cups fresh strawberries or raspberries
- 2 cups ice cubes
- 2 tablespoons honey
- 1 tablespoon lemon juice

DIRECTIONS

1 Put strawberries or raspberries, ice cubes, honey, and lemon juice into the blender.

2 Cover blender with the lid and blend on high speed about 1 minute or until mixture is slushy. Turn off blender. Pour drink into glasses. Use rubber scraper to get all of the drink out of the blender. Makes 4 servings.

Nutrition Facts per serving: 56 calories, 0 g total fat, 0 mg cholesterol, 3 mg sodium, 15 g carbohydrate, 2 g fiber, 1 g protein.

MAKE IT YOURS USE FRESH BLUEBERRIES OR BLACKBERRIES INSTEAD OF STRAWBERRIES.

SHOW SOME SPARKLE SIPPERS

MUSIC DIRECTOR DEE LA DUKE LIKES CAMPERS TO ADD A LITTLE SPARKLE TO EVERYTHING THEY DO. SHE WOULD LOVE THESE SPARKLY DRINKS!

UTENSILS

- Large pitcher with lid
- Measuring cups
- Wooden spoon
- Serving glasses

INGREDIENTS

- 1 envelope (0.28-ounce) low-calorie cherry-flavored drink mix
- 1 cup orange juice
- 1 2-liter bottle carbonated water, chilled
  Ice cubes

DIRECTIONS

1 Put the drink mix into the pitcher. Pour in the orange juice; stir with the wooden spoon until mixed. Cover and chill until serving time.

2 Just before serving, carefully pour the carbonated water into the juice mixture.

3 Fill glasses with ice cubes. Pour the juice mixture into the glasses. Makes 10 servings.

Nutrition Facts per serving: 13 calories, 0 g total fat, 0 mg cholesterol, 43 mg sodium, 3 g carbohydrate, 0 g fiber, 0 g protein.

MAKE IT YOURS USE PUNCH-FLAVORED SOFT DRINK MIX IN PLACE OF THE CHERRY-FLAVORED SOFT DRINK MIX.

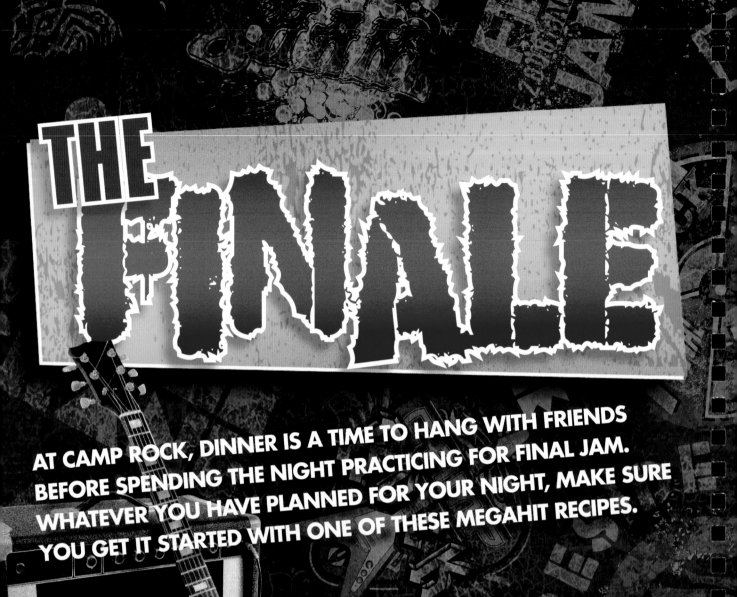

THE FINALE

AT CAMP ROCK, DINNER IS A TIME TO HANG WITH FRIENDS BEFORE SPENDING THE NIGHT PRACTICING FOR FINAL JAM. WHATEVER YOU HAVE PLANNED FOR YOUR NIGHT, MAKE SURE YOU GET IT STARTED WITH ONE OF THESE MEGAHIT RECIPES.

POP STAR TOSTADAS

THIS ISN'T JUST ANY TOSTADA. IT HAS POP STAR STATUS—LOADED WITH TACO FLAVOR AND TOPPED WITH LETTUCE AND CHEESE.

UTENSILS

- Large skillet
- Wooden spoon
- Colander
- Medium bowl
- Disposable container
- Measuring cups
- Baking sheet
- Hot pads
- Wire cooling rack

INGREDIENTS

12 ounces lean ground beef

⅔ cup fresh or bottled salsa

6 tostada shells

1 cup shredded reduced-fat cheddar cheese

½ to 1 cup purchased shredded lettuce

1 medium tomato, chopped

Light dairy sour cream (optional)

Bottled salsa (optional)

DIRECTIONS

1 Turn on oven to 375°F. Put the ground beef in the large skillet. Break up meat with the wooden spoon. Put the skillet on a burner. Turn the burner to medium-high heat. Cook until meat is brown, stirring now and then with the wooden spoon. This will take 8 to 10 minutes. Turn off burner. Remove skillet from burner.

2 Place the colander over the bowl. Spoon meat mixture into the colander and let fat drain into the bowl. Spoon meat back into skillet. Put fat into the disposable container and throw away. Stir the ⅔ cup salsa into meat in skillet.

3 Arrange the tostada shells on the baking sheet. Spoon the meat mixture onto the shells. Sprinkle with the cheese. Put the baking sheet in the oven. Bake about 10 minutes or until the cheese is melted. Turn off oven.

4 Use the hot pads to take the baking sheet out of the oven. Set baking sheet on the wire rack. Sprinkle the tostadas with the lettuce and tomato. If desired, top each with sour cream and additional salsa. Makes 6 servings.

Nutrition Facts per serving: 218 calories, 13 g total fat, 47 mg cholesterol, 385 mg sodium, 9 g carbohydrate, 1 g fiber, 18 g protein.

MAKE IT YOURS INSTEAD OF TOPPING TOSTADA SHELLS, PLACE MEAT MIXTURE, CHEESE, LETTUCE, AND TOMATO IN WHOLE WHEAT FLOUR TORTILLAS AND ROLL UP FOR A QUICK BURRITO.

NEVER DRY CHICKEN

WHEN TESS FINDS OUT THAT MITCHIE'S MOM IS THE CAMP COOK, SHE COMPLAINS THAT THE CHICKEN IS TOO DRY. BUT SHE CAN'T MAKE THAT COMPLAINT ABOUT THIS CHICKEN. IT'S COATED IN BARBECUE SAUCE.

UTENSILS

- Measuring cups
- Medium mixing bowl
- 2 wooden spoons
- Foil
- Small saucepan
- Hot pads
- Serving plate
- Large spoon

INGREDIENTS

3 cups packaged shredded cabbage with carrot (coleslaw mix)

⅓ cup bottled reduced-calorie ranch salad dressing

2 cups shredded cooked chicken*

½ cup bottled barbecue sauce

6 whole wheat hamburger buns, split

Dill pickle slices (optional)

DIRECTIONS

1 Put the coleslaw mix and ranch salad dressing in the medium bowl. Use a wooden spoon to stir until combined. Cover the bowl with foil and refrigerate until ready to serve.

2 Put the chicken and the barbecue sauce into the small saucepan. Put saucepan on a burner. Turn burner to medium heat. Cook and stir with wooden spoon until mixture is hot. Turn burner off. Use hot pads to remove saucepan from burner.

3 Place bottom halves of the hamburger buns on a serving plate. Use the large spoon to put chicken mixture on the bun bottoms. Cover with bun tops. Serve with coleslaw and, if desired, pickle slices. Makes 6 sandwiches.

*Tip: For shredded chicken, use a purchased roasted chicken. Pull the meat from the chicken, discarding skin and bones. Use 2 forks to pull chicken into shreds.

Nutrition Facts per serving: 272 calories, 8 g total fat, 45 mg cholesterol, 626 mg sodium, 32 g carbohydrate, 3 g fiber, 18 g protein.

MAKE IT YOURS HALVE THREE 6-INCH WHOLE WHEAT PITA BREAD ROUNDS. SPOON CHICKEN MIXTURE INTO PITA HALVES.

BAND FAVORITE CALZONES

THREE FAVORITE PIZZA INGREDIENTS COMBINE TO MAKE THESE CHART-TOPPING CALZONES. THEY'RE EVEN BETTER DIPPED IN PIZZA SAUCE.

UTENSILS

- Baking sheet
- Foil
- Large cutting board
- Sharp knife
- Pizza cutter or sharp knife
- Measuring cups
- Measuring spoons
- Pastry brush
- Hot pads
- Wire cooling rack
- Wide metal spatula

INGREDIENTS

Nonstick cooking spray
3 ounces Canadian-style bacon
All-purpose flour (1 to 2 teaspoons)
1 13.8-ounce package refrigerated pizza dough
⅓ cup pizza sauce
1 cup shredded part-skim mozzarella cheese
1 tablespoon low-fat milk
1 tablespoon finely shredded Parmesan cheese
Pizza sauce (optional)

DIRECTIONS

1 Turn on the oven to 400°F. Line the baking sheet with foil and lightly coat with nonstick cooking spray. Save until Step 4. Put the Canadian bacon on the cutting board. Use the sharp knife to chop the meat. Remove meat from cutting board. Save until Step 3.

2 Sprinkle the cutting board with a little flour. Unroll the pizza dough into a rectangle on the cutting board. Using the pizza cutter or sharp knife, cut the dough rectangle in half lengthwise, then cut each half into thirds crosswise. You should have 6 rectangles.

3 Use the small spoon to spread some of the ⅓ cup pizza sauce onto each dough rectangle. Sprinkle 1 side of each dough rectangle with some of the mozzarella cheese and some of the Canadian bacon. Fold the other side of each dough rectangle over the cheese and Canadian bacon. Use the fork to seal the edges. Prick the top of each with the fork several times. Use the pastry brush to brush the top of each calzone with milk and sprinkle with Parmesan cheese.

4 Arrange the calzones on the baking sheet. Put the baking sheet in the oven. Bake for 12 minutes or until golden brown. Turn off oven. Use the hot pads to remove the baking sheet from the oven. Put baking sheet on the wire rack. Cool calzones on baking sheet for about 10 minutes. Use the spatula to remove the calzones from the baking sheet. Serve warm with additional pizza sauce, if desired. Makes 6 servings.

Nutrition Facts per serving: 212 calories, 7 g total fat, 20 mg cholesterol, 559 mg sodium, 26 g carbohydrate, 1 g fiber, 11 g protein.

MAKE IT YOURS USE REDUCED-FAT CHEDDAR OR SWISS CHEESE IN PLACE OF THE MOZZARELLA CHEESE.

SPICY COMEBACKS PIZZA

CAITLYN LIKES TO KEEP THINGS INTERESTING WITH HER FREQUENT ONE-LINERS, OFTEN EXPRESSED AFTER ONE OF TESS' INSULTS. YOU CAN KEEP DINNER INTERESTING BY TRYING THIS BARBECUE CHICKEN PIZZA.

UTENSILS

- 15x10x1-inch baking pan
- Measuring cups
- Large spoon
- Hot pads
- Wire cooling rack
- Pizza cutter

INGREDIENTS

Nonstick cooking spray

1 13.8-ounce package refrigerated pizza dough

½ cup bottled barbecue sauce

1 9-ounce package refrigerated cooked chicken breast strips

1 medium red sweet pepper, cut into thin strips

½ cup shredded reduced-fat cheddar cheese

Snipped fresh cilantro leaves (optional)

DIRECTIONS

1 Turn on the oven to 400°F. Coat the 15x10x1-inch baking pan with nonstick cooking spray. Using your hands, unroll the pizza dough and press with fingers to form a 12x8-inch rectangle. Pinch edges of dough to form crust.

2 Use the spoon to carefully spread the barbecue sauce over the crust. Top with the chicken breast strips and red pepper strips. Sprinkle with the cheese.

3 Put pan in the oven. Bake for 13 to 18 minutes or until crust is brown and cheese melts. Turn off oven. Use hot pads to remove baking pan from oven. Let stand on cooling rack for 5 minutes. Use the pizza cutter to cut pizza into squares. If desired, sprinkle servings with cilantro. Makes 6 servings.

Nutrition Facts per serving: 259 calories, 6 g total fat, 35 mg cholesterol, 761 mg sodium, 33 g carbohydrate, 2 g fiber, 17 g protein.

MAKE IT YOURS INSTEAD OF THE CHICKEN BREASTS, USE 1 POUND GROUND TURKEY, COOKED AND DRAINED.

WORLD FAMOUS BURGERS

WHEN MITCHIE FINDS OUT SHE'S GOING TO CAMP ROCK, HER DAD IS MAKING HIS FAMOUS TORRES BURGERS. GIVE THEM A TRY!

UTENSILS

- Measuring cups
- Measuring spoons
- Large bowl
- Wooden spoon
- Broiler pan
- Pancake turner
- Hot pads
- Serving plate

INGREDIENTS

¼ cup fine dry bread crumbs

2 tablespoons bottled barbecue sauce

¼ teaspoon salt

⅛ teaspoon black pepper

1 pound uncooked ground turkey or chicken

4 whole wheat hamburger buns, split

4 romaine or green leaf lettuce leaves

4 fresh or canned pineapple slices

Bottled barbecue sauce (optional)

DIRECTIONS

1 Turn on the oven to broil.* Put the bread crumbs, 2 tablespoons barbecue sauce, salt, and pepper in the large bowl. Put the ground turkey in the bowl and stir with the wooden spoon until well mixed. Use your hands to divide the meat into 4 equal portions. Shape each portion into a flat, round patty that measures about 3½ inches across.

2 Place turkey patties on the unheated rack of a broiler pan. Broil 4 to 5 inches from the heat for 14 to 18 minutes or until no pink color is left in the burgers (165°F), turning once with the pancake turner halfway through broiling.* Use hot pads to remove the pan from the oven.

3 Place bottom halves of the hamburger buns on a serving plate. Place a lettuce leaf on the bottom of each bun. Use the pancake turner to lift burgers from broiler pan and set them on the lettuce leaves. Place a pineapple slice on top of each burger. If desired, add additional barbecue sauce. Cover with bun tops. Makes 4 servings.

*Note: Broilers are really hot so have an adult help you with it. Also ask an adult to use a meat thermometer to make sure the burgers are fully cooked.

Nutrition Facts per serving: 351 calories, 11 g total fat, 90 mg cholesterol, 737 mg sodium, 38 g carbohydrate, 3 g fiber, 25 g protein.

MAKE IT YOURS USE KETCHUP IN PLACE OF BARBECUE SAUCE. OMIT THE PINEAPPLE SLICES AND TOP BURGERS WITH TOMATO SLICES.

FOOD FIGHT PASTA

TESS AND CAITLYN USED IT FOR A FOOD FIGHT, BUT SPAGHETTI IS BEST EATEN WITH A REALLY GOOD TOMATO SAUCE. SO SKIP THE FOOD FIGHT AND ENJOY YOUR PASTA WITH THIS DELICIOUS HOMEMADE SAUCE.

UTENSILS

- Large saucepan
- Hot pads
- Colander
- Measuring spoons
- Medium saucepan
- Wooden spoon
- 6 dinner plates
- Large spoon
- Measuring cups

INGREDIENTS

10 ounces dried multigrain spaghetti

1 14½-ounce can diced tomatoes, undrained

1 15-ounce can tomato sauce

2 tablespoons tomato paste

1 teaspoon dried Italian seasoning, crushed

Dash ground black pepper

¼ cup grated Parmesan cheese

DIRECTIONS

1 Cook spaghetti in the large saucepan according to the package directions. When spaghetti is cooked, turn off the burner. Use the hot pads to remove the pan from the burner. Place the colander in the sink. Pour spaghetti into the colander to drain water.

2 While the spaghetti cooks, put the undrained tomatoes, tomato sauce, tomato paste, Italian seasoning, and pepper in the medium saucepan. Use the wooden spoon to combine.

3 Place the saucepan on the burner. Turn the burner to medium-low heat. Cook until heated through, stirring occasionally. Turn off the burner. Use the hot pads to remove the pan from the burner.

4 Divide spaghetti among six dinner plates. Spoon tomato sauce over spaghetti. Sprinkle with Parmesan cheese. Makes 6 servings.

Nutrition Facts per serving: 219 calories, 2 g total fat, 3 mg cholesterol, 496 mg sodium, 44 g carbohydrate, 5 g fiber, 9 g protein.

MAKE IT YOURS ADD 1 CUP OF YOUR FAVORITE COOKED VEGETABLES TO THE SAUCE.

TACO NIGHT TACOS

THE CAMPERS LOVE TACO NIGHT AND SO WILL YOU WHEN YOU TRY THESE CHICKEN TACOS. BE SURE TO TRY DIFFERENT TOPPERS.

UTENSILS

- Measuring cups
- Medium saucepan
- Wooden spoon
- Hot pads
- Waxed paper
- Table knife
- Serrated knife

INGREDIENTS

2 cups chopped cooked chicken

1 cup bottled salsa

6 7- to 8-inch whole wheat flour tortillas

½ cup canned fat-free refried beans

2 cups shredded lettuce

1 medium tomato, chopped

½ cup finely shredded reduced-fat cheddar cheese and/or Monterey Jack cheese

Salsa (optional)

DIRECTIONS

1 Put the chicken and 1 cup salsa in the saucepan. Use the wooden spoon to combine. Put the saucepan on a burner. Turn the burner to medium heat. Cook chicken mixture, stirring now and then with the wooden spoon until heated through. Turn off burner. Use hot pads to remove saucepan from burner.

2 Place a piece of waxed paper on counter or table. Spread the tortillas out on waxed paper. Spread refried beans over tortillas with the table knife. Arrange chicken mixture on each tortilla near one edge. Top chicken with lettuce, tomato, and cheese.

3 Roll up tortillas, starting from the edge nearest the filling. Use the serrated knife to cut each tortilla roll in half crosswise. If desired, serve with additional salsa. Makes 6 servings.

Nutrition Facts per serving: 271 calories, 9 g total fat, 47 mg cholesterol, 728 mg sodium, 21 g carbohydrate, 12 g fiber, 26 g protein.

MAKE IT YOURS FOR EXTRA SPICE, ADD ONE 4-OUNCE CAN DICED GREEN CHILI PEPPERS, DRAINED, TO THE SAUCEPAN WITH THE CHICKEN AND SALSA.

DON'T BE SLOPPY JOES

SHANE'S UNCLE BROWN IS ALWAYS URGING HIM TO CLEAN UP HIS ACT. THAT MAY NOT BE SO EASY WITH THESE SAUCY SANDWICHES!

UTENSILS

- Large skillet with a lid
- Wooden spoon
- Colander
- Medium bowl
- Disposable container
- Measuring spoons
- Measuring cups
- Serrated knife
- Small spoon

INGREDIENTS

12 ounces lean ground beef
1 8-ounce can tomato sauce
1 tablespoon dried minced onion
¼ teaspoon dried oregano, crushed
¼ teaspoon dried basil, crushed
8 3-inch whole wheat hard rolls
1 cup shredded part-skim
  mozzarella cheese (4 ounces)
Carrot sticks (optional)

DIRECTIONS

1 Put the ground beef in the skillet. Break up meat with the wooden spoon. Put the skillet on a burner. Turn the burner to medium-high heat. Cook until meat is completely browned, stirring now and then with the wooden spoon. This will take 8 to 10 minutes. Turn off burner. Remove skillet from burner.

2 Place the colander over the bowl. Spoon meat into the colander and let fat drain into the bowl. Spoon meat back into skillet. Put fat in the disposable container and throw away.

3 Add the tomato sauce, onion, oregano, and basil to meat mixture in the skillet. Put the skillet on a burner. Turn the burner to medium-high heat. Cook until the mixture comes to boiling, stirring now and then with the wooden spoon. Turn the burner to low heat. Cover and cook for 15 minutes. Turn off burner.

4 Use the serrated knife to cut a thin slice from the top of each roll; set tops of rolls aside. Use the spoon to scoop out insides of rolls, leaving ½-inch thick shells. Set shells aside. Reserve scooped-out bread for another use.

5 Spoon beef mixture evenly into bread shells. Top with mozzarella cheese. Cover with the roll tops. If desired, serve with carrot sticks. Makes 8 servings.

Nutrition Facts per serving: 224 calories, 7 g total fat, 35 mg cholesterol, 451 mg sodium, 23 g carbohydrate, 2 g fiber, 15 g protein.

MAKE IT YOURS USE 12 OUNCES GROUND TURKEY OR CHICKEN IN PLACE OF GROUND BEEF.

ENCORE

THE END OF FINAL JAM IS THE HIGHLIGHT OF CAMP ROCK.
IT'S THE PERFECT WAY TO END THE SUMMER. AND THESE
DESSERTS ARE THE PERFECT WAY TO END YOUR MEAL.
YOU MIGHT RECOGNIZE SOME OF THESE SWEET TREATS—
THEY'RE FROM CONNIE'S OWN CAMP COOKBOOK.

PLATINUM CD COOKIES

CONNIE MAKES MUSIC-INSPIRED TREATS FOR THE CAMPERS, LIKE THESE CD COOKIES. YOU CAN PERSONALIZE THEM WITH YOUR SONG TITLES.

UTENSILS

- Measuring cups
- Medium mixing bowl
- Electric mixer
- Measuring spoons
- Rubber scraper
- Wooden spoon
- Rolling pin
- 3½- to 4-inch round cookie cutter
- Cookie sheet
- Hot pads
- Pancake turner
- Wire cooling rack

INGREDIENTS

¼ cup butter, softened
¼ cup sugar
½ teaspoon baking powder
⅛ teaspoon salt
1 egg white
1 teaspoon vanilla
1¼ cups all-purpose flour
1 tube black decorator icing

DIRECTIONS

1 Turn on the oven to 375°F. Put butter in the mixing bowl. Beat butter with the electric mixer on medium speed for 30 seconds. Add sugar, baking powder, and salt. Beat until combined, stopping the mixer occasionally and scraping the side with the rubber scraper. Add the egg white and vanilla and beat until combined. Beat in as much of the flour as you can with the mixer. Stop the mixer. Stir in any remaining flour with the wooden spoon. Use your hands to shape the dough into a ball.

2 On a lightly floured surface, use the rolling pin to roll dough to ¹⁄₁₆ to ⅛ inch thick. Cut into rounds with cookie cutter. Transfer cookies to an ungreased cookie sheet, leaving about 1 inch between cookies.

3 Put cookie sheet in oven. Bake for 6 to 8 minutes or until cookie edges are very lightly browned. Use the hot pads to remove cookie sheet from oven. Use the pancake turner to transfer cookies to the cooling rack. Repeat with remaining dough. Turn off oven. Cool cookies completely.

4 Use the black decorator icing to design and personalize your own CD. If desired, serve with apple slices. Makes 8 cookies.

Nutrition Facts per cookie: 170 calories, 7 g total fat, 15 mg cholesterol, 112 mg sodium, 23 g carbohydrate, 1 g fiber, 3 g protein.

MAKE IT YOURS CORE AN APPLE. SLICE APPLE CROSSWISE INTO ¼-INCH-THICK SLICES. USE THE BLACK DECORATOR ICING TO DESIGN AND PERSONALIZE YOUR OWN (APPLE) CD.

AWARD WINNING BROWNIES

CELEBRATE PEGGY'S (MARGARET'S) BIG FINAL JAM WIN WITH THESE RICH, CHOCOLATE BROWNIES.

UTENSILS

- 9x9x2-inch baking pan
- Medium saucepan
- Wooden spoon
- Hot pads
- Measuring cups
- Measuring spoons
- Rubber scraper
- Wooden toothpick
- Wire cooling rack

INGREDIENTS

Nonstick cooking spray
¼ cup butter
⅔ cup granulated sugar
½ cup cold water
1 cup all-purpose flour
¼ cup unsweetened cocoa powder
1 teaspoon baking powder
¼ cup mini semisweet chocolate pieces
¼ cup dried blueberries
2 teaspoons sifted powdered sugar (optional)

DIRECTIONS

1 Turn on the oven to 350°F. Lightly coat the bottom of the 9x9x2-inch baking pan with nonstick cooking spray. Save until Step 4.

2 Put butter in the medium saucepan. Place the saucepan on the burner. Turn burner to low heat. Cook until butter is melted. Stir frequently with the wooden spoon. Turn off the burner. Use the hot pads to remove the saucepan from the burner.

3 Use the wooden spoon to stir the granulated sugar and water into the melted butter until combined. Stir in the flour, cocoa powder, and baking powder and then the chocolate pieces and dried blueberries.

4 Spoon batter into prepared pan, spreading evenly with the wooden spoon. Use the rubber scraper to scrape all the batter out of the saucepan.

5 Put the pan in the oven. Bake for 15 minutes or until a wooden toothpick comes out clean. (To test doneness, use the hot pads to pull out oven rack. Stick a toothpick in the center of the brownies; pull out the toothpick. If any brownie sticks to it, bake a few minutes more; test again.) Turn off oven. Use the hot pads to remove the baking pan from the oven. Place the pan on the wire rack to cool. If desired, sprinkle brownies with powdered sugar. Makes 16 brownies.

Nutrition Facts per serving: 122 calories, 4 g total fat, 8 mg cholesterol, 37 mg sodium, 20 g carbohydrate, 1 g fiber, 1 g protein.

MAKE IT YOURS STIR ¼ CUP PEANUTS OR CHOPPED WALNUTS INTO THE BATTER WITH THE CHOCOLATE PIECES AND BLUEBERRIES.

AFTER FINAL JAM PIZZA

THIS CARAMEL APPLE PIZZA IS GREAT TO EAT ON A COOL NIGHT BY A WARM CAMPFIRE, OR AFTER HOSTING YOUR OWN FINAL JAM PARTY.

UTENSILS

- 12-inch pizza pan
- Hot pads
- Wire cooling rack
- Measuring cups and spoons
- 2 small mixing bowls
- Wire whisk
- Wooden spoon
- Small saucepan
- Small spoon
- Pizza cutter

INGREDIENTS

½ of a 15-ounce package rolled refrigerated unbaked piecrust (1 crust)

½ cup light caramel apple dip

¼ cup light dairy sour cream

3 tablespoons all-purpose flour

1 apple, cored and thinly sliced

3 tablespoons packed brown sugar

½ teaspoon ground cinnamon

¼ cup light caramel apple dip

DIRECTIONS

1 Turn on the oven to 375°F. Let the piecrust sit at room temperature for 15 minutes. Unroll piecrust onto a 12-inch round pizza pan. Use your fingers to press piecrust to edge of pan. Place the pan in the oven. Bake for 12 minutes or until crust is golden brown. Use the hot pads to remove the pan from the oven. Place the pan on the wire rack. Cool on wire rack for 15 minutes.

2 Put the ½ cup caramel dip, sour cream, and flour in the small bowl and mix with the wire whisk. Use a table knife to spread caramel mixture over cooled baked piecrust. Arrange apple slices over caramel layer. Put the brown sugar and cinnamon in another small bowl and mix with the wooden spoon. Use your fingers to sprinkle sugar mixture over apple slices.

3 Use hot pads to put pizza pan back in oven. Bake 15 minutes more or until apples are tender. Turn off the oven. Use the hot pads to remove the pan from the oven and place on the wire rack. Cool for 15 minutes.

4 Put the ¼ cup caramel dip in the small saucepan. Place the pan on the burner. Turn the burner to medium heat. Heat just until warm. Turn off the burner. Use the hot pads to remove the pan from the burner. Use the small spoon to drizzle the caramel dip over the pizza. Use the pizza cutter to cut pizza into wedges. Serve warm. Makes 10 servings.

Nutrition Facts per serving: 193 calories, 7 g total fat, 7 mg cholesterol, 136 mg sodium, 34 g carbohydrate, 1 g fiber, 2 g protein.

MAKE IT YOURS USE ONE MEDIUM PEAR, CORED AND THINLY SLICED, IN PLACE OF THE APPLE.

EIGHTH NOTE CUPCAKES

HERE'S ANOTHER ONE OF CONNIE'S CAMP DESSERTS. THEY TASTE GREAT BUT ALSO HELP YOU REMEMBER YOUR NOTES.

UTENSILS

- Muffin pans with 2½-inch cups
- Paper bake cups
- Hot pads
- Wire cooling rack
- Table knife
- Wooden toothpicks

INGREDIENTS

1 16.75-ounce package confetti angel food cake mix

1 16-ounce can white frosting

1 tube black decorator icing with plastic writing tip

Fresh fruit, optional

DIRECTIONS

1 Turn on the oven to 375°F. Follow the cupcake directions on the cake mix package to prepare and bake the cupcakes in paper bake cups. Turn off the oven. Use the hot pads to remove the pans from the oven. Cool cupcakes in the pans on the wire rack. Remove the cupcakes from the pans.

2 Use the knife to spread the tops of the cooled cupcakes with the white frosting. Use a wooden toothpick to trace the eighth note image into the frosting. Retrace using black decorator icing and plastic writing tip. Garnish with fresh fruit, if desired. Makes 30 cupcakes.

Nutrition Facts per serving: 129 calories, 3 g total fat, 0 mg cholesterol, 159 mg sodium, 24 g carbohydrate, 0 g fiber, 1 g protein.

MAKE IT YOURS USE ANY FLAVOR TWO-LAYER CAKE MIX.

PRODUCE A HIT CRISP

MOST CRISPS ARE MADE WITH BUTTER BUT THIS ONE USES PEANUT BUTTER, SO IT WILL REALLY TOP THE CHARTS WITH YOUR FRIENDS.

UTENSILS

- 2-quart square baking dish
- Measuring spoons
- Small mixing bowl
- Wooden spoon
- Foil
- Hot pads
- Wire cooling rack
- Measuring cups
- Medium mixing bowl

INGREDIENTS

6 medium cooking apples, cored, and thinly sliced
2 tablespoons all-purpose flour
1 tablespoon packed brown sugar
⅔ cup quick-cooking rolled oats
2 tablespoons all-purpose flour
2 tablespoons packed brown sugar
¼ cup peanut butter
2 tablespoons chopped peanuts

DIRECTIONS

1 Turn on the oven to 375°F. Put the apple slices in the 2-quart square baking dish. Put 2 tablespoons of flour and 1 tablespoon brown sugar in the small bowl. Use the wooden spoon to stir together until well combined. Use your fingers to sprinkle the flour mixture evenly over the apples in the dish. Use the wooden spoon to stir the apples until they are coated with the flour mixture. Cover baking dish with foil.

2 Put covered dish in oven. Bake for 15 minutes. Use hot pads to remove baking dish from oven. Let stand on a cooling rack with foil cover in place.

3 Put rolled oats, 2 tablespoons flour, and 2 tablespoons brown sugar in a medium bowl. Use a fork to stir the peanut butter into the flour mixture until mixture resembles coarse crumbs. Use the wooden spoon to stir in the peanuts.

4 Uncover the apple mixture. Use your fingers to sprinkle the oat mixture over the apples. Use hot pads to put baking dish back in the oven (uncovered). Bake for 15 minutes more or until apples are tender and topping is golden. Turn off oven. Use hot pads to remove baking dish from oven. Let stand on cooling rack. Serve warm. Makes 8 servings.

Nutrition Facts per serving: 166 calories, 6 g total fat, 0 mg cholesterol, 46 mg sodium, 27 g carbohydrate, 3 g fiber, 4 g protein.

MAKE IT YOURS ADD ¼ CUP RAISINS OR DRIED CHERRIES TO THE BAKING DISH WITH THE APPLES.

BEACH JAM CAMPFIRE S'MORES

IT WOULDN'T BE CAMP WITHOUT S'MORES. MAKE YOUR OWN AT HOME—NO CAMPFIRE REQUIRED—AND YOU'LL BE SINGING "TOO COOL" BEFORE YOU KNOW IT.

UTENSILS

- Scissors
- Small spoon

INGREDIENTS

- 1 package 100-calorie bear-shape cinnamon graham snack cookies
- ½ of a 100-calorie container ready-to-eat chocolate pudding*
- 6 tiny marshmallows

DIRECTIONS

1 Open the package of crackers. Use the scissors to cut off more of the top of the package to make it easier to eat with a spoon. Spoon the pudding on top of the crackers in bag. Top with the marshmallows. Makes 1 serving.

*Note: Cover the remaining pudding and chill it in the refrigerator for up to 3 days.

Nutrition Facts per serving: 160 calories, 4 g total fat, 0 mg cholesterol, 226 mg sodium, 30 g carbohydrate, 1 g fiber, 2 g protein.

MAKE IT YOURS

SUBSTITUTE A PACKAGE OF CINNAMON GRAHAM CRACKER CRISPS FOR THE BEAR-SHAPE CINNAMON GRAHAM SNACK COOKIES.

BEACH JAM

TIRED OF BEING BACKUP BOWLS

DON'T THINK OF FRUIT AS A BACKUP DESSERT WHEN COOKIES AND CAKE AREN'T AN OPTION. INSTEAD, LET IT LEAD AS A STAR DESSERT, AS IT DOES HERE WITH A LITTLE PUDDING.

UTENSILS

- Measuring cups
- Large mixing bowl
- Wire whisk
- Large spoon

INGREDIENTS

- 1 4-serving-size package instant lemon pudding mix
- 1⅓ cups low-fat milk
- 1½ cups fresh blueberries and/or raspberries
- 4 waffle ice cream bowls or large waffle ice cream cones
- ¼ cup low-fat granola

DIRECTIONS

1 Put pudding mix and milk in the large bowl. Whisk about 2 minutes or until smooth and mixture starts to thicken.

2 Divide fruit among the waffle bowls or cones. Top with pudding. Sprinkle with granola. Makes 4 servings.

Nutrition Facts per serving: 233 calories, 3 g total fat, 4 mg cholesterol, 411 mg sodium, 50 g carbohydrate, 3 g fiber, 4 g protein.

MAKE IT YOURS USE INSTANT VANILLA OR CHOCOLATE PUDDING WITH SLICED BANANAS.

FREEZE THAT NOTE

PEGGY, AND OTHER GOOD SINGERS, CAN HOLD A NOTE A LONG TIME. BUT SHE CAN'T HOLD THIS CAMP TREAT FOR LONG OR IT WILL MELT.

UTENSILS

- Measuring cups
- Small saucepan
- Wooden spoon
- Hot pads
- Electric blender
- 3-quart rectangular baking dish
- Foil
- Ice cream scoop
- 10 dessert dishes

INGREDIENTS

¾ cup water

⅓ cup sugar

3 cups seeded watermelon cubes

2 cups halved strawberries

Fresh strawberries (optional)

DIRECTIONS

1 Put water and sugar in the small saucepan. Use the wooden spoon to combine. Place the saucepan on the burner. Turn the burner to medium-high heat. Cook and stir with the wooden spoon until boiling. Continue to boil for 2 minutes. Turn off the burner. Use the hot pads to remove the saucepan from the burner. Cool the mixture in the saucepan for 15 minutes.

2 Place the watermelon and 2 cups strawberries in the blender. Cover the blender with the lid and blend on high speed until nearly smooth. Turn off the blender. Pour the warm syrup into the blender. Cover the blender with the lid and blend on high speed until smooth.

3 Pour the watermelon mixture into a 3-quart rectangular baking dish. Cover with foil and freeze about 3 hours or until almost firm.

4 Remove the dish from the freezer. Using a fork, break up the frozen fruit mixture until almost smooth but not melted. Cover and freeze for 2 hours or overnight, or until completely frozen.

5 Remove the dish from the freezer. Let stand at room temperature for 30 minutes. Use the ice cream scoop to scrape mixture and spoon into dessert dishes. If desired, top with fresh strawberries. Makes 10 servings.

Nutrition Facts per serving: 49 calories, 0 g total fat, 0 mg cholesterol, 1 mg sodium, 12 g carbohydrate, 1 g fiber, 1 g protein.

MAKE IT YOURS USE 2 CUPS SLICED, PEELED KIWIFRUIT IN PLACE OF THE STRAWBERRIES. GARNISH WITH KIWIFRUIT SLICES.

INDEX

AUTOGRAPHS 101

IF YOU'RE GOING TO BE A ROCK STAR, YOU HAVE TO GET USED TO SIGNING YOUR AUTOGRAPH FOR FANS. BUT WHAT TYPE OF AUTOGRAPH WILL YOU USE? TRY SIGNING YOUR NAME WITH THESE SUGGESTIONS AND THEN PICK THE ONE YOU LIKE BEST. OR COMBINE TECHNIQUES TO REALLY MAKE THE AUTOGRAPH YOURS.

★ Make the first letter of your first and last name bigger than the other letters.

_____

★ Add a curve, circle, or long, straight line to the end of your first and last name.

_____

★ Sign only your first name, adding a shape at the end.

_____

★ Add a shape or symbol instead of a dot over any i's in your name.

_____

★ Sign your first name and then just the last letter of your name followed by a squiggly line.

_____

★ Print just your first name, in regular or block letters.

_____

★ Try something that is unique to you (such as an eighth note in place of an "s" to show you love music).

_____

WHAT DID YOU COME UP WITH? WRITE YOUR FINAL AUTOGRAPH HERE AND THEN KEEP PRACTICING IT SO YOU'LL BE READY FOR STARDOM.